Preface

In the world of trucking, where the open road
meets the bottom line, success is not simply a
matter of driving from point A to point B. It's a
complex dance of strategy, negotiation, and
perseverance. Drawing inspiration from Robert
Greene's timeless work, "The 48 Laws of
Power," we present the "48 Laws of Trucking" -
a guide for those who navigate the highways
and byways of the trucking industry.
Each law encapsulates a principle, a strategic
maneuver, or a mindset essential for
triumphing in this demanding field. From
owner-operators to drivers to fleet managers,
these laws offer insights to help you not only
survive but thrive in the fiercely competitive
world of trucking.
Armed with these laws, you will learn to
navigate the challenges, seize opportunities,
and steer your trucking endeavors towards
success. Embrace these laws, and let the road
ahead be paved with strategic victories.

Table of Contents

Introduction:

Trucking is a business that requires grit, perseverance, and a strategic mindset to succeed. In this book, we'll explore the 48 Laws of Trucking, influenced by Robert Greene's 48 Laws of Power, and how they can be applied to the trucking industry. Whether you're an owner-operator, company driver, or a fleet manager, these laws will help you navigate the competitive and challenging world of trucking.

Law 1: Never outshine the shipper

When dealing with a shipper, it's important not to outshine them. While it's essential to be efficient and professional, you don't want to make the shipper feel insignificant or threatened. They hold the power in the transaction, and you must respect that.

Example: You're picking up a load from a shipper known for their strict procedures. Instead of trying to rush the process, you patiently follow their instructions, showing respect for their protocols. By doing so, you create a positive impression, ensuring a smooth transaction and leaving a lasting professional relationship.

Law 2: Control the load, control the power

In the world of trucking, the load is everything. If you control the load, you control the power. Ensure that you have a reliable and efficient system for loading and unloading cargo to maximize your power in the industry.

Example: You're transporting delicate artwork for a prestigious gallery. Taking charge of every aspect, you personally oversee the loading, implement specialized security measures, and carefully monitor the climate control. Your meticulous attention ensures the artwork arrives in perfect condition, solidifying your reputation as a trusted carrier for high-value cargo.

Law 3: Make your own rules

Trucking is a business that requires flexibility and adaptability. Don't be afraid to make your own rules when it comes to scheduling, pricing, and routes. Take control of your business and make decisions that work best for you.

Example: Presented with an unconventional delivery request, you negotiate a tailored approach. By leveraging your expertise, you propose a unique route that shaves off significant transit time while complying with regulations. Your creative solution not only impresses the client but also sets a precedent for future collaborations.

Law 4: Never reveal your hand

Keep your plans and strategies to yourself. Never reveal your hand to your competitors. They will use any information they can get to gain an advantage over you.

Example: In a negotiation with a broker, you strategically withhold your willingness to adjust rates. Instead, you carefully probe for information about the shipment's urgency and the client's budget constraints. This allows you to make a counteroffer that maximizes your profit while still meeting the client's needs.

Law 5: Always have a backup plan

In trucking, unexpected problems are bound to happen. Always have a backup plan in place to handle any issues that may arise. Being prepared will ensure that you stay ahead of the competition.

Example: En route to a delivery, you receive news of a major traffic incident ahead. Without hesitation, you reroute using your pre-planned alternative, avoiding the delay and ensuring an on-time delivery. Your foresight and preparedness save the day, impressing both the client and the dispatcher.

Law 6: Be wary of brokers

Brokers can be an essential part of the trucking industry, but they can also be a hindrance. Be wary of brokers who try to undercut your rates or take advantage of your services. Always negotiate your terms and don't be afraid to walk away from a deal that doesn't work for you.

Example: While working with a new broker, you conduct thorough research, checking their reputation and verifying their track record. When negotiating rates, you stand firm, ensuring your compensation aligns with industry standards. Your caution and diligence protect your interests in the transaction.

Law 7: Know your worth

Don't undervalue your services. Know your worth and charge accordingly. Don't be afraid to negotiate with shippers and brokers to get the rates you deserve.

Example: When presented with a load that requires specialized equipment and handling, you confidently provide a fair rate that reflects the unique demands of the job. Your self-assured approach communicates your value and expertise, garnering respect from both the shipper and broker.

Law 8: Keep your equipment in top condition

Your equipment is the backbone of your business. Keep it in top condition to ensure that it runs smoothly and efficiently. Regular maintenance and repairs are essential to prevent breakdowns and delays.

Example: Regular maintenance is a cornerstone of your business. By adhering to a strict schedule and addressing any potential issues promptly, your truck remains reliable and efficient. This dedication to upkeep minimizes the risk of breakdowns, ensuring smooth operations and timely deliveries.

Law 9: Stay ahead of the competition

The trucking industry is highly competitive. Stay ahead of the competition by staying up to date with industry trends and technology. Adopt new strategies and tools to increase efficiency and profitability.

Example: Recognizing the shift towards sustainable practices in the industry, you invest in eco-friendly technologies for your fleet. This forward-thinking approach not only reduces operational costs but also positions your business as a leader in environmentally conscious transportation solutions.

Law 10: Build strong relationships

Building strong relationships with shippers, brokers, and other industry professionals is essential to success in trucking. Cultivate these relationships through open communication and reliable service.

Example: Over the years, you've cultivated a network of trusted industry contacts, from shippers to fellow drivers. When faced with a challenging situation, such as unexpected weather delays, you leverage these relationships to find alternative solutions and ensure the cargo reaches its destination on time.

Law 11: Stay organized

Trucking requires a high level of organization. Keep track of your schedules, invoices, and paperwork to ensure that you don't miss any important deadlines.

Example: Your meticulous record-keeping system allows you to track every aspect of your business, from schedules and expenses to maintenance logs. This organized approach enables you to quickly access critical information, make informed decisions, and maintain a high level of professionalism in all your operations.

Law 12: Never stop learning

The trucking industry is constantly evolving. Never stop learning and seeking out new information to stay ahead of the curve. Attend industry events and training sessions to stay informed about new technologies and best practices.

Example: Recognizing the growing importance of digital tools in the industry, you invest time in learning advanced logistics software. This knowledge empowers you to optimize routes, track shipments in real-time, and provide clients with accurate, up-to-the-minute information about their cargo.

Law 13: Be patient

Trucking can be a frustrating business at times. Be patient and remain calm in the face of setbacks and challenges. A level head and a positive attitude will help you navigate any difficulties that come your way.

Example: When facing a slow period with fewer available loads, you resist the urge to take on low-paying jobs out of desperation. Instead, you wait for the right opportunity that aligns with your rates and expertise. This patience pays off, as you secure a high-value contract that boosts your earnings.

Law 14: Embrace change

Change is inevitable in the trucking industry. Embrace it and be willing to adapt to new technologies, regulations, and business models. Don't be afraid to take risks.

Example: As regulations evolve, you proactively adapt your operations to comply with new safety standards. This willingness to embrace change not only keeps your business legally compliant but also demonstrates your commitment to the well-being of your drivers and the public.

Law 15: Play the long game

Trucking is a long-term game. Don't focus on short-term gains at the expense of your long-term success. Build sustainable business practices that will carry you through the ups and downs of the industry.

Example: Rather than pursuing quick, one-off transactions, you focus on building long-term partnerships with reliable shippers. By consistently providing exceptional service and demonstrating your commitment to their success, you secure repeat business and become their preferred carrier for future shipments.

Law 16: Maintain a strong reputation

In the trucking industry, your reputation is everything. Maintain a strong reputation by providing reliable and efficient service. Word-of-mouth referrals can make or break your business.

Example: Your reputation for reliability and professionalism precedes you. Shippers and brokers seek out your services because they know they can trust you to deliver on time and without incident. This strong reputation not only leads to a steady flow of business but also allows you to negotiate favorable terms

Law 17: Know your limitations

Don't take on more than you can handle. Know your limitations and don't overextend yourself. Overcommitment can lead to delays, accidents, and other problems that can harm your business.

Example: When presented with an opportunity for a cross-country haul with an unrealistic deadline, you carefully assess the situation. Recognizing that safety and compliance are non-negotiable, you decline the load, explaining your limitations to the broker. This decision preserves your integrity and prevents potential risks associated with an impossible timeline.

Law 18: Choose your partners wisely

Your business partners can make or break your success. Choose partners wisely and thoroughly vet them before entering into any business agreements. Don't be afraid to walk away from a partnership that doesn't align with your values or goals.

Example: When considering a partnership with a new carrier, you conduct a thorough evaluation of their safety record, equipment, and financial stability. This diligence ensures that you align yourself with a reliable and reputable partner, minimizing the risk of complications or setbacks in your joint operations.

Law 19: Be adaptable

Trucking requires adaptability. Be willing to change your plans on the fly to accommodate unexpected issues or opportunities. A flexible mindset will help you navigate the unpredictable nature of the industry.

Example: Faced with sudden changes in weather conditions, you quickly adjust your route and schedule to ensure safe travel. Your ability to adapt to unforeseen circumstances not only prevents delays but also showcases your professionalism and commitment to cargo safety.

Law 20: Don't burn bridges

In the trucking industry, you never know who you might need in the future. Don't burn bridges with shippers, brokers, or other industry professionals. Always maintain a professional and respectful demeanor, even in difficult situations.

Example: Even when faced with a challenging client or partner, you maintain a professional and courteous demeanor. You address any issues or concerns diplomatically, seeking resolution rather than escalating conflicts. This approach preserves your reputation and leaves the door open for potential future collaborations.

Law 21: Use technology to your advantage

Technology can be a powerful tool in the trucking industry. Use it to increase efficiency, streamline processes, and stay ahead of the competition. Embrace new technologies and seek out innovative solutions to common industry challenges.

Example: Implementing a modern fleet management system allows you to monitor driver behavior, optimize routes, and track maintenance schedules. This technology-driven approach increases operational efficiency, reduces costs, and positions your business at the forefront of innovation in the industry.

Law 22: Stay informed about regulations

Trucking is a heavily regulated industry. Stay informed about changes to regulations that could impact your business. Failure to comply with regulations can lead to fines, penalties, and even the loss of your operating license.

Example: You make it a priority to regularly review and understand the latest regulatory changes, from hours-of-service requirements to emissions standards. By staying informed and ensuring compliance, you protect your business from potential fines and legal complications while demonstrating your commitment to safety and responsibility.

Law 23: Don't underestimate the power of communication

Clear and effective communication is essential in the trucking industry. Keep your shippers, brokers, and other partners informed about any issues or delays. Prompt communication can help you avoid costly mistakes and maintain strong relationships.

Example: In a situation where unexpected traffic delays occur, you promptly notify your dispatcher and the client. You provide regular updates on your estimated time of arrival, allowing them to adjust their plans accordingly. Your proactive communication demonstrates transparency and professionalism, building trust with both parties.

Law 24: Emphasize safety

Safety should always be a top priority in the trucking industry. Invest in training, equipment, and other resources to ensure that your drivers are prepared to handle any situation. A focus on safety can help you avoid accidents and maintain a positive reputation.

Example: Safety is at the forefront of your operations. You conduct regular safety training sessions for your drivers, ensuring they are well-prepared to handle any situation on the road. Additionally, you invest in advanced safety technology, such as collision avoidance systems, to further protect your drivers and the cargo they transport.

Law 25 : Build a good working relationship with your dispatcher

As a truck driver, your dispatcher is your lifeline to the rest of the company. Building a good working relationship with your dispatcher is essential to ensuring that you have the support you need to succeed on the road. Communicate clearly and effectively, provide regular updates on your progress, and be open to feedback and constructive criticism. A strong relationship with your dispatcher can help you stay on top of your workload, manage your time effectively, and ultimately deliver better service to your clients.

Example: You maintain open lines of communication with your dispatcher, providing them with updates on your progress and any challenges you encounter. In return, they prioritize your assignments and work to accommodate your preferences whenever possible. This collaborative relationship ensures a smooth workflow and enhances your overall efficiency.

Law 26 : Take care of yourself on the road

Driving a truck can be a physically and mentally demanding job. It's important to take care of yourself to ensure that you stay healthy and productive on the road. Get plenty of rest, eat a balanced diet, and exercise regularly. Take breaks throughout the day to stretch your legs and clear your mind. Keep your cab clean and organized to reduce stress and promote a positive working environment. By taking care of yourself, you'll be better equipped to handle the challenges of the road and deliver top-notch service to your clients.

Example: Recognizing the importance of physical well-being, you prioritize a balanced diet and regular exercise during your stops. You also make time for relaxation and ensure you get enough rest to prevent fatigue. By taking care of yourself, you maintain the physical and mental stamina required for safe and efficient driving.

Law 27: Be patient with payments

Payment delays are common in the trucking industry. Be patient and persistent in your efforts to collect payment from shippers and brokers. Establish clear payment terms upfront to avoid misunderstandings.

Example: You've delivered a crucial shipment for a valued client who, due to unforeseen circumstances, faces a temporary cash flow issue. Instead of immediately applying pressure for payment, you open a line of communication, expressing understanding and offering flexible terms. This patience not only strengthens your client relationship but also positions you as a trusted partner, likely to be prioritized in future transactions. Remember, in the world of trucking, patience can be a powerful tool for building lasting, mutually beneficial partnerships.

Law 28: Keep your eyes on the road

In the trucking industry, distractions can be dangerous. Keep your focus on the road and avoid distractions such as texting, eating, or talking on the phone. A single mistake can have serious consequences.

Example: You're on a long-haul journey through challenging terrain, and distractions abound. Your phone buzzes with notifications, but you resist the urge to check it. Instead, you stay focused on the road, adjusting your speed and maintaining a safe following distance. Your unwavering attention prevents potential accidents and ensures the safety of both yourself and fellow drivers. By embodying this law, you demonstrate the utmost commitment to safety, setting a standard of excellence for all who share the road with you. Remember, in the world of trucking, keeping your eyes on the road is not just a rule; it's a life-saving principle.

Law 29: Stay financially disciplined

Trucking can be a capital-intensive business. Stay financially disciplined by carefully managing your cash flow and investing in the areas of your business that will generate the most return on investment.

Example: In the face of economic fluctuations, you maintain a steadfast commitment to financial discipline. Instead of succumbing to the temptation of unnecessary expenditures, you meticulously track expenses, renegotiate contracts, and explore cost-saving measures. This discipline allows you to weather economic challenges while keeping your business on a solid financial foundation. By embodying this law, you position yourself as a resilient and financially savvy player in the competitive world of trucking. Remember, in the world of trucking, financial discipline is the key to long-term stability and success.

Law 30 : Don't be afraid to ask for help and offer it when needed

As a truck driver or a trucking business owner, you may encounter situations where you need help or support from others. Don't be afraid to ask for help when you need it. Whether it's a breakdown on the road, a complex logistical challenge, or a personal issue that's affecting your work, seeking assistance from colleagues, friends, or professionals can be a crucial step in overcoming the problem and getting back on track.

Example: On a cross-country journey, you encounter an unexpected mechanical issue with your truck. Instead of attempting a risky roadside repair, you reach out to a fellow driver from a neighboring company known for their expertise. They not only offer guidance but also connect you with a reliable mechanic in the area. Grateful for the assistance, you make a mental note to reciprocate the favor in the future. This exchange of support not only gets you back on the road safely but also strengthens the sense of camaraderie within the trucking community.

Law 31: Build strong relationships

Building strong relationships with shippers, brokers, and other industry professionals can pay off in the long run. Nurture these relationships by staying in touch and showing appreciation for their business. You never know when you might need their help in the future.

Example: Over the years, you've cultivated a deep and mutually beneficial relationship with a key shipper. You consistently go above and beyond to ensure their cargo is delivered safely and on time. In return, they prioritize your loads, offer you preferential rates, and even recommend your services to their industry peers. This strong relationship not only secures a steady stream of business but also provides a foundation of trust and reliability in the competitive world of trucking. Remember, in the world of trucking, building strong relationships is not just a strategy; it's a cornerstone of success.

Law 32: Anticipate problems

Trucking is full of potential problems, from traffic delays to mechanical issues. Anticipate these problems and have a plan in place to address them quickly and effectively. This will help you minimize the impact of these issues on your business.

Example: As you plan a complex multi-stop delivery route through unpredictable weather conditions, you take proactive steps to anticipate potential challenges. You double-check weather forecasts, identify alternative routes, and ensure your drivers are equipped with the necessary safety gear. This foresight pays off when unexpected storms hit, allowing you to swiftly adjust routes and schedules, ultimately ensuring the safe and on-time delivery of the cargo.

Law 33: Stay organized

Organization is key to success in the trucking industry. Keep detailed records of all transactions, maintain an up-to-date schedule, and keep your equipment and paperwork in order. This will help you stay on top of your business and avoid costly mistakes.

Example: In your bustling trucking business, you implement a comprehensive logistics management system. This system tracks shipments, schedules maintenance, and manages driver assignments efficiently. When a client requests a last-minute change to a delivery, you consult your organized system, quickly reassign drivers, and update schedules without missing a beat.

Law 34: Learn from your mistakes

Mistakes are inevitable in any business, but it's important to learn from them. Analyze your mistakes and make changes to your processes to avoid repeating them in the future. Don't dwell on your mistakes - instead, use them as an opportunity to improve.

Example: After a shipment encounters an unexpected delay due to a logistical oversight, you conduct a thorough post-mortem analysis. You identify the root cause, implement new procedures to prevent similar issues in the future, and communicate the lessons learned to your team. This experience becomes a catalyst for positive change, leading to improved processes and heightened attention to detail in your operations.

Law 35: Embrace competition

Competition can be fierce in the trucking industry, but it can also be a source of motivation. Embrace competition and use it to drive you to improve your services, expand your reach, and stay ahead of the curve.

Example: Instead of viewing other carriers as rivals, you seek opportunities for collaboration. You join an industry consortium that allows carriers to share resources and expertise for more efficient operations. By working together, you collectively bid on larger contracts and offer comprehensive solutions to clients. This collaborative approach not only strengthens your position in the market but also fosters a spirit of camaraderie within the industry.

Law 36: Don't compromise on safety

Safety is non-negotiable in the trucking industry. Don't compromise on safety for any reason, even if it means sacrificing profits or losing a client. Your reputation and the well-being of your drivers are too important to put at risk.

Example: You receive a rush order for a time-sensitive delivery, but the requested timeline would require your driver to exceed legal driving hours. Instead of succumbing to the pressure to meet the deadline at the expense of safety, you communicate the situation to the client. You propose an alternative schedule that ensures compliance with regulations and prioritizes the well-being of your driver.

Law 37: Build a strong team

Building a strong team is essential to success in the trucking industry. Hire experienced and reliable drivers, invest in their training and development, and create a positive and supportive work environment. A strong team will help you deliver top-notch service and maintain a competitive edge.

Example: You invest in comprehensive training programs for your drivers, focusing not only on technical skills but also on soft skills like communication and customer service. Through mentorship and regular feedback, you foster a culture of continuous learning and growth. As a result, your team members take pride in their work, exhibit a strong sense of camaraderie, and consistently deliver exceptional service to your clients.

Law 38: Stay on top of industry trends

The trucking industry is constantly evolving. Stay on top of industry trends by attending conferences, reading industry publications, and networking with other professionals. This will help you stay ahead of the curve and adapt to changes in the market.

Example: You regularly attend industry conferences, subscribe to industry publications, and actively participate in online forums dedicated to the trucking industry. This commitment to staying informed about the latest advancements and emerging technologies allows you to integrate cutting-edge solutions into your operations.

Law 39: Emphasize customer service

Customer service is a key differentiator in the trucking industry. Emphasize excellent customer service by responding promptly to inquiries, providing regular updates, and going above and beyond to meet the needs of your clients.

Example: A client contacts you with a specific request for temperature-controlled transportation of sensitive pharmaceuticals. You not only ensure that the cargo is meticulously handled and monitored for temperature fluctuations but also provide regular updates on its status. Additionally, you offer personalized solutions to accommodate any special requirements.

Law 40: Don't let setbacks derail you

Setbacks are inevitable in any business, but it's important not to let them derail you. Stay focused on your goals and keep moving forward, even in the face of adversity. A positive attitude and a persistent mindset can help you overcome any obstacle.

Example: While on a critical delivery route, you encounter an unexpected road closure due to a major accident. Instead of panicking, you calmly assess the situation, consult your navigation system for alternative routes, and notify the client of the delay. With a clear head and a determined spirit, you reroute and continue on, eventually reaching the destination safely and only slightly behind schedule. Your ability to adapt and persevere in the face of adversity not only ensures the successful completion of the delivery but also showcases your resilience and determination as a trusted carrier.

Law 41: Network effectively

Networking is essential to success in the trucking industry. Attend industry events, join professional organizations, and connect with other professionals on social media. Building strong relationships with other industry players can help you uncover new opportunities, stay up-to-date on industry news, and even find potential partners or clients.

Example: You actively participate in industry conferences, workshops, and networking events. At a recent conference, you strike up a conversation with a representative from a major shipping company. By discussing your expertise in specialized cargo and sharing success stories, you establish a connection built on mutual interest and trust.

Law 42: Leverage technology

Technology has revolutionized the trucking industry, and savvy operators are using it to their advantage. Use GPS tracking, electronic logging devices, and other technology to improve efficiency, reduce costs, and enhance safety. Embracing technology can help you stay competitive and deliver top-notch service.

Example: You invest in state-of-the-art telematics and IoT devices for your fleet. These technologies provide real-time data on vehicle performance, driver behavior, and cargo conditions. When a client inquires about the status of their shipment, you're able to provide precise, up-to-the-minute information, instilling confidence in your reliability. Additionally, the data collected allows you to analyze and optimize routes, leading to cost savings and increased efficiency.

Law 43: Be adaptable

The trucking industry is constantly changing, and it's important to be adaptable. Stay flexible and open to new ideas, be willing to pivot your business strategy as needed, and embrace new technologies and trends. Being adaptable can help you stay ahead of the curve and thrive in a rapidly evolving industry.

Example: You're on a long-haul trip when you receive an urgent message from a client requesting an unscheduled stop to pick up additional cargo. Without hesitation, you reroute your journey, adjust your schedule, and coordinate with the client to ensure a seamless pickup. Your adaptability not only meets the client's immediate needs but also demonstrates your agility and commitment to going above and beyond.

Law 44: Manage risk

Risk management is a key part of any successful trucking operation. Assess potential risks, such as accidents or equipment failures, and develop plans to mitigate them. Invest in insurance coverage to protect your business and drivers, and stay up-to-date on safety regulations and compliance requirements.

Example: You meticulously review each potential shipment, assessing factors like cargo type, distance, and weather conditions. For high-value or sensitive cargo, you insist on additional security measures and insurance coverage. Additionally, you conduct thorough background checks on any new partners or carriers you consider working with.

Law 45: Know your strengths and weaknesses

Knowing your strengths and weaknesses can help you make better business decisions. Play to your strengths by focusing on the services and routes where you excel, and look for ways to improve in areas where you may be weaker. Understanding your strengths and weaknesses can help you stay competitive and build a more successful business.

Example: After careful analysis, you realize that your company excels in handling time-sensitive, high-value cargo. You make the strategic decision to focus your marketing efforts on industries that require expedited deliveries, such as pharmaceuticals and electronics. For long-haul freight, you establish partnerships with carriers specializing in those routes, creating a mutually beneficial network. This approach allows you to maximize efficiency and profitability by concentrating on areas where you have a competitive advantage.

Law 46: Embrace innovation

Innovation is key to staying ahead in the trucking industry. Look for new ways to improve your processes, explore new technologies, and be open to trying new approaches. Embracing innovation can help you stand out from the competition and deliver better service to your clients.

Example: Recognizing the industry's shift towards sustainability, you invest in a fleet of hybrid trucks and implement a robust recycling program at your facilities. This innovative approach not only reduces your environmental impact but also positions your business as a forward-thinking leader in eco-friendly transportation. Additionally, you explore cutting-edge logistics software that optimizes routes, leading to fuel savings and increased efficiency.

Law 47: Manage your finances effectively

Effective financial management is essential to running a successful trucking business. Keep detailed financial records, create a budget, and monitor your cash flow closely. Invest in equipment and technology wisely, and consider outsourcing tasks like accounting or payroll to save time and money.

Example: In response to fluctuating fuel prices, you implement a fuel efficiency program that includes driver training on economical driving techniques and regular maintenance to ensure optimal engine performance. Additionally, you closely monitor expenses, negotiate favorable contracts with suppliers, and leverage technology for accurate financial reporting.

Law 48: Be resilient

Finally, resilience is key to success in the trucking industry. The road can be tough, but a resilient mindset can help you weather the ups and downs of the industry. Stay positive, be persistent, and never give up on your goals. With the right mindset and a commitment to excellence, you can build a thriving trucking business that stands the test of time.

Example: Faced with a sudden disruption in the supply chain due to unforeseen circumstances, you swiftly pivot your operations. You tap into alternative sourcing options, adjust delivery routes, and communicate transparently with clients about potential delays. Your ability to adapt to changing circumstances and maintain business continuity showcases your resilience and determination.

Conclusion: Navigating the Road Ahead

In the dynamic world of trucking, where every mile holds the potential for triumph or challenge, the wisdom encapsulated in the "48 Laws of Trucking" serves as your compass. These laws, drawn from the timeless principles of strategy and power, are the cornerstone of success for trucking professionals and businesses alike.

As you've journeyed through these laws, you've learned the art of negotiation, the importance of adaptability, and the power of strategic foresight. You've discovered how to build strong relationships, prioritize safety, and leverage technology for a competitive edge. You've witnessed the impact of resilience, the value of innovation, and the necessity of effective financial management.

Remember, these laws are not static decrees, but dynamic guidelines to be applied judiciously in the ever-evolving landscape of the trucking industry. By internalizing these principles and weaving them into the fabric of your operations, you stand poised to navigate the road ahead with confidence and strategic acumen.

In the realm of trucking, success is not a singular destination but a continuous journey of growth, adaptation, and excellence. Embrace these laws, and let them be the foundation upon which you build a legacy of success in the trucking industry.

Safe travels, and may every mile be a testament to the power of strategic mastery in the world of trucking.

www.ingramcontent.com/pod-product-compliance
Lightning Source LLC
Chambersburg PA
CBHW060006300526
45794CB00003B/1115

48 LAWS OF TRUCKING

D.C. ROLLINS

ISBN 9798864514818

90000

9 798864 514818